The Mindf

"Of all the tools that salon professionals have at their fingertips, The *Mindful Beauty Maker's Little Book Of Wisdom* is one of the most vital. Within its beautifully designed pages, the messages, affirmations and activities when put into action, empower body, mind and spirit.These three are the core of enduring energy offering a lifetime of creative fulfillment in and out of the salon." —**ANN MINCEY, VICE PRESIDENT GLOBAL COMMUNICATIONS (RETIRED), REDKEN 5TH AVENUE NYC**

"*The Mindful Beauty Maker's Little Book Of Wisdom* is a great tool for building self esteem in an industry that can give so much of themselves to others, yet can somehow still feel unworthy." —**KEVIN MURPHY KEVIN MURPHY HAIR**

"In a world where a woman's sense of self worth is an impossible puzzle of internal conflict, based on an external expectation of perfection, it's no wonder the beauty industry's revenue is expected to exceed $62 billion in 2016 according to market research. But to what end? Andrea Snyder's commitment to inspiring a movement of beauty making as an internal, versus simply external journey, gives hope to future generations of women. As an expert on authentic leadership, I can personally attest to the level of conscious love Andrea devotes to her clients, leaving them feeling beautiful on the inside and out. I trust this book will touch many lives!" —**KATHLEEN O'GRADY, CEO, RALEIGH COACHING ACADEMY**

"What a delightful book. It's all you need to build an emotionally successful daily practice in the salon and beyond." —**ALLEN O'BARR, MD PSYCHIATRIST, DIRECTOR OF COUNSELING AT UNC, CHAPEL HILL**

"Andrea has created the perfect life companion for the giving, talented beauty maker. With beautiful art and gentle encouraging words this guide has it all. Part inspiration, part action plan and part journal this guide will empower those who use it to live a more balanced and peaceful existence. Use daily, weekly or monthly to find your own personal zen! I can't wait to get started myself." —**MARY WILSON, DESTINATION REJUVENATION, WILSON EDUCATIONAL PRODUCTIONS INC. SINGING BOWL SISTERS**

"The beauty and wellness industry needs to spend more time teaching from the *Little Book of Wisdom*. Skill is only half a service providers success the other half is spelled out beautifully within these pages." —**SEBASTIAN STEELE, FOUNDER OF PRO PRODUCT DISTRIBUTOR AND FIRE SALONS, GREENSBORO & BURLINGTON, NC**

"Andrea helped me get started in this wonderful industry—always upbeat and positive, she showed me at the start of my career how to build my confidence as an artist and grow my independence as a professional. Today, as a freelance artist with recognized contributions to the industry, I always reflect back on Andrea's inspiration—a mentor for all artists!" —**ERICA KEELAN REYNOLDS , NAHA COLOR FINALIST, OWNER STUDIO SAGE, JACKSONVILLE, FL**

THE MINDFUL BEAUTY MAKER'S

Little Book of Wisdom

a chair side inspirational guide for salon & spa pros and their clients

Andrea Saccone Snyder

Design/Production: Lesley Landis Designs, www.lesleylandis.com
Cover Image: "Beauty Within" ©2016 by Andrea Saccone Snyder
All interior illustrations by Andrea Saccone Snyder

www.theflowbeautyproject.com
www.themindfulbeautymaker.com
Contact Andrea Saccone Snyder by email at:
snydera71@gmail.com

gratitude

I am in extreme gratitude to my husband, David, and my son, Greyson. Your unending support of my neverending creative endeavors does not go unnoticed. But hey, it takes one to know one as artists go. You both kept the house in order literally and figuratively. Dave, you are my best friend and creative inspiration. Greyson, you are my heart and soul, and I love you — all that you are and are yet to become. Thank you, Dad (Joseph Saccone) for always seeing the beauty in me and in others. You taught me kindness. I know how proud you are of me 'cause I feel you in spirit. Big love to my big bros, Joe and Paul. (Hey, your lil' sis is an author!)

I owe my passion for the beauty industry to my wise and beautiful mother, Paulette, and my late grandmother Josephine. You both are with me every day in the salon. Standing at both of your sides, I learned everything I know of beauty and compassion, and for that I am forever grateful.

I thank my bosses, mentors, teachers, coaches and colleagues in the beauty biz and beyond. I have learned something of value from each and every one of you. I hope you know who you are. If I have had the pleasure of having your soul in my beauty making chair, then I have learned from and am grateful to you as well!

Thank you, Craig Kayser and Cindy Campbell, for believing in me and fueling my creativity. Thank you, Vicky Kim, for your genius left brain editing and your right brain too. You pulled it all together in the end. Thank you to the brilliant and talented Lesley Landis for your unique artistic eye and for capturing just the right look for this little book. You rock!

I would also like to thank all the wonderful stylists and beauty pros who I've had the pleasure of working with in my salon over the years.

I am the luckiest girl in the world to have landed in a place where I have found the most precious soul tribe of sister love I could have ever dreamed of—Shamanmamma Sharon, and the 7 Sisters! Cathy (Brooksie), Sheila, Roxanne, Amy, Andi, and Janice. You have each given me a piece of your authentic beauty and wisdom to share in these pages. You have encircled me with love, support and the courage to fly beyond what my solo vision would let me see. Thank you from the bottom of my heart.

And to all my other sisterhoods of friends, you know who you are and I thank you.

In beauty, Andrea xo

inspiration

"It is my considered opinion that the hairdresser is the most influential person in any community. When the public goes to a hairdresser, something happens to them. They feel safe, they relax. The hairdresser knows what their skin is like under the makeup, they know their age, they don't have to keep up any kind of pretense. People tell a hairdresser things they wouldn't dare confess to a priest and they are open about matters they'd try to conceal from a doctor. When people place their secret lives in the hairdresser's hands, the hairdresser gains an authority few other people attain. I have heard hairdressers quoted with complete conviction on art, literature, politics, economics, child care and morals. I tell you that a clever, thoughtful, ambitious hairdresser wields a power beyond comprehension of most people."

JOHN STEINBECK,

EXCERPT FROM *MY TRAVELS WITH CHARLIE IN SEARCH OF AMERICA*

Hair dyes are not intended for
temporary tattoos may increa
not be applied on customers: a
ns to coloring products b) wh
athological condition (eczema
gated to inform the consum
le contraindications,
: Apply in a well
vironment a
itivity to
n. It is
earm

…messen, mit dem spezifischen Oxida…
…on waschen
Haut auftragen und trocknen lassen. Den Testst…
…hen auf der Haut belassen. Wenn es zu keiner Haut…
…werden. Im Fall einer allergischen Reaktion Nicht a…
…ei späteren Anwendungen nicht zu allergischen Rea…
…ötungen, Juckreiz oder Ausschlag den betreffenden…
…t nicht weiter verwenden. Vor erneuter Verwend…
…he Verstärkung der allergischen Reaktion zu ve…
Colorationscreme in einem nichtmetallischen…
…ten Artego Peroxide O2: 3% (10 Vol.) nur bei Ve…
…% (20 Vol.) deckt graue Haare ab und hellt bis zu 2…
…und hellt bis zu 3 Tonhöhen auf. 40 vol. (12%)…
…bis 40 Minuten. **Anwendung:** immer auf das tro…
…für Haar, das noch nie gefärbt wurde: Tragen Sie di…
…der Haare auf. Beginnen Sie ca. 2–3 cm entfernt…
…einwirken, dann tragen Sie die Farbe am Ansatz auf…
…einwirken. **Für Haar, das bereits gefärbt wurde:** Tra…
…die Farbe 25-30 Minuten einwirken. Wenn notwendig…
…er und tragen die Farbcreme auf die Längen und Spitz…
…10 Minuten einwirken oder noch besser gleichen Sie d…
…Semi-Permanent (Tönung) Sortiment ohne Ammoniak…
…Handbuch). **Shampoonieren:** Spülen Sie die Creme mit warme…
…und shampoonieren Sie das Haar anschließend mit Arteg…
…**grauen Haaren:** 100… …e Deckkraft erreichen Sie imme…
…Cold Natural Nua… …tion kurz… Verwendung von Mo…
…den Vor dem Auftragen ist Beispiel…
…gilt auch für Kunden, die bereits…
…inen kleinen Bereich in der Ellbogen…
…ocken tupfen
…ine kleine Menge des Produkts…
…schließend dem gewünschten Farbt…
…ine kleine Menge der Mischung auf d…
…aschen oder abdecken
…ie Mischung 48 Stunden ununterbro…
…ommt, kann das Produkt angewendet…
…Test ist keine Garantie dafür, dass es…
…treten kann. Bei Hautreaktionen wie…
…möglich abspülen und das Produ…
…dukts einen Arzt auf…
…**ischungsverhältnis:** Mischen Sie die…
…ichen Teilen (1:1) mit dem gewünscht…
…Tönung, hellt bis zu 1 Tonhöhe auf…
…9% (30 Vol.) deckt graue Haare ab…
…onhöhen auf. **Einwirkungszeit:** 30…
…ftragen, niemals vorher waschen. F…
…f die mittleren Längen und Spitze…
…ssen Sie die Farbe 20-25 Minuten…
…Creme weitere 30-35 Minuten…
…e am Ansatz auf und lassen Si…
…ie restliche Farbe mit Was…
…die Coloration weiter…
…denselben…

…op allergische reacti…
…klanten die: a) eerder…
…ucten b) een gevoelige, geïrr…
…aandoening hebben (eczeem…
…informeren over de inhoud van…
…risico op mogelijke …ische rea…
…ruimte en de benodigde voorbere…
…een goede veiligheid. Gebruik zor…
…in gevoeligheid voor de product…
…wordt voorgesteld geschikte han…
…aanbrengen, de posetijd en met…
…zorgvuldig gereinigd…
…g. Als u medische onderzoek…
…overgevoeligheid voor een…
…innen veroorzaken. Bewaar de verf…
…ondervindt.
…dige gevoeligheidstest Wij raden…
…ndeling te doen, zelfs met klanten die…
…klein gedeelte in de elleboog of achter het…
…ak een kleine hoeveelheid van de verf klaar…
…vold door het kleur recept dat u wilt gebruiken…
…eng een kleine hoeveelheid van het kleur…
…gedeelte niet wassen of afdekken en laten rus…
…de substantie 48 uur zitten. Als de huid…
…deling toepassen. Als er wel een reactie…
…ur niet dat er geen allergische…
…gen. Als de huid een allergi…
…k de huid schoonmaken en…
…odig bent, voordat u kleurt…
…te beperken. **Gebruik:** De…
…in gelijke delen (1:1)…
…en maak tot 1 klein…

How to Use This Book

I have written this book for you — the lover of beauty, the visionary, the creator of possibilities. It is meant to be a chair side guide and source of inspiration for you and your clientele. As you read please insert your unique title and work situation where you see the term "stylist" or "hairdresser", as this book can serve as a guide for any service provider.

If you are new to the world of beauty, WELCOME! You are sure to gain valuable insight into the deep growth that is possible for you in your new career! If you are mid-career or an old pro, my intent is to inspire you to find fresh insight about who you are behind the chair and how you can lead others to embrace whole beauty.

Of the bountiful concepts on which I could write, I have selected the topics which have been essential for me in cultivating a balanced and meaningful practice, both inside and outside the salon. I provide some exercises and questions so you can reflect, a space to make notes or journal about them, and integrate the topics into your own practices when you have a bit of time to sit quietly and explore. Carve out time to get a chapter accomplished before sleep and integrate the work in your dreams. Set aside time on a day off and go to the park or a coffee shop with this book and your journal in tow, for some "you time". Knock out a chapter or two and get inspired for the week ahead! Keep this book with you in the salon so that when you need your daily dose of inspiration, these affirmations and reminders are at your fingertips. It might be helpful to write down the affirmations on a separate sheet of paper and keep your favorites somewhere in your home where you can say them out loud often.

It is my pure joy to share with you what I have learned by being a conscious witness and an intentional contributor to the world of beauty. It is my deepest hope that you will be inspired and awakened to your own true nature and to your gifts as a maker of beauty, and that you will pass this wisdom on to those you touch everyday.

xo, *Andrea*

Hair dyes are not intended for
emporary tattoos may increa
t be applied on customers: a
s to coloring products b) wh
thological condition (eczema,
ated to inform the consum
contraindications,
Apply in a wel
ironment a
tivity to
. It is
arm

ammeßen mit dem spezifischen Oxidat
on mischen.
Haut auftragen und trocknen lassen. Den Test
hen auf der Haut belassen. Wenn es zu keiner Haut
werden. Im Fall einer allergischen Reaktion Nicht a
ei späteren Anwendungen nicht zu allergischen Re
stungen, Juckreiz oder Ausschlag den betreffende
t nicht weiter verwenden. Vor erneuter Verwend
ne Verstärkung der allergischen Reaktion zu ve
Colorationscreme in einem nichtmetallischen
ten Artégo Peroxide O2: 3% (10 Vol.) nur bei Ve
(20 Vol.) deckt graue Haare ab und hellt bis zu 2
und hellt bis zu 3 Tonhöhen auf; 40 vol. (12%)
bis 40 Minuten. **Anwendung:** immer auf das tro
ür Haar, das noch nie gefärbt wurde: Tragen Sie di
der Haare auf. Beginnen Sie ca. 2–3 cm entfernt
nwirken, dann tragen Sie die Farbe am Ansatz auf
nwirken. **Für Haar, das bereits gefärbt wurde:** Tra
die Farbe 25-30 Minuten einwirken. Wenn notwendig
er und tragen die Farbcreme auf die Längen und Spitz
5-10 Minuten einwirken oder noch besser gleichen Sie di
dem Semi-Permanent (Tönung) Sortiment ohne Ammoniak
Handtuch). **Shampoonieren:** Spülen Sie die Creme mit warm
t, und shampoonieren Sie das Haar anschließend mit Artégo
von grauen Haaren: 100 ... Deckkraft erreichen Sie imme
... Verwendung von Mo
Cold Natural Nua
den vor dem Auftragen ist. Beispiel
gilt auch für Kunden die bereits
nen kleinen Bereich in der Ellbogen
rocken tupfen.
ne kleine Menge des Produkts
nschließend dem gewünschten Farbt
ne kleine Menge der Mischung auf d
aschen oder abdecken.
ie Mischung 48 Stunden ununterbro
ommt, kann das Produkt angewendet
r Test ist keine Garantie dafür, dass es
men kann. Bei Hautreaktionen wie
verzüglich abspülen und das Produ
einen Arzt auf
chungsverhältnis: Mischen Sie da
ichen Teilen (1:1) mit dem gewünschten
Tönung, hellt bis zu 1 Tonhöhe auf
; 9% (30 Vol.) deckt graue Haare ab
onhöhen auf. **Einwirkungszeit:** 30
ftragen, niemals vorher waschen.
f die mittleren Längen und Spitzen
sen Sie die Farbe 20-25 Minuten
Creme weitere 30-35 Minuten
e am Ansatz auf und lassen S
restliche Farbe mit Was
en die Coloration weiter

that, in rare cases, may
e reaction
ersons under 16 years ol
se the risk of allergic reactions. T
) who previously have had a
ose scalp is sensitive, irrit
psoriasis, facial
ut the co

op allergische reactie
klanten die: **a)** eerder
ducten **b)** een gevoelige, geïrr
aandoening hebben (eczeem
informeren over de inhoud van
risico op mogelijke ... sche reac
ruimte en de benodigde voorber
een goede veiligheid. Gebruik
in gevoeligheid voor de product
wordt voorgesteld geschikte han
aanbrengen, de posetijd en met
de haar
zorgvuldig gereinigd.
. Als u medische onderzoek
overgevoeligheid voor een
innen veroorzaken. Bewaar de
ondervindt.
dige gevoeligheidstest. Wij raden
deling te doen, zelfs met klanten die
ein gedeelte in de elleboog of achter het
een kleine hoeveelheid van de verf kle
door het kleur recept dat u wilt gebruiken
Breng een kleine hoeveelheid van het kleur rec
gedeelte niet wassen of afdekken en laten rus
de substantie 48 uur zitten. Als de hu
deling toepassen. Als er wel een reactie
niet dat er geen allergische re
egen. Als de huid een allergi
de huid schoonmaken
ig bent, voordat u kleur
te beperken. **Gebruik:** De
in gelijke delen (1:1)
en maakt tot 1 kleu

indingen treffen voor een
er de noodzakelijke vo
en met consequenties o
schoenen te dragen d
Als mogelijk
Vermijd werkmater
werkmaterialen.

What exactly is a Beauty Maker?

You might be asking yourself this question.

Simply put, a Beauty Maker is a male or female salon professional, including but not limited to: a hair stylist, colorist, barber, esthetician, makeup artist, body worker, energy healer, guest/client specialist, who understands that the connections you create with your clients day to day, year to year, decade to decade, run much deeper than just a haircut, a hair color or salon service. These connections can lead to enormous personal and spiritual enhancement for both the client and the professional. The Beauty Maker honors this potential and strives to be of service in the making of whole beauty— in yourself, your client and your little piece of the world behind the chair.

The Beauty Maker's Mission

A Beauty Maker is more than just a hairdresser or salon pro. A hairdresser simply does hair. A Beauty Maker is an alchemist, an artist, a visionary and an inner/outer or whole beauty guide. A Beauty Maker can see what is below the surface of your client, what is hidden from the casual onlooker. A Beauty Maker's mission is to not only help clients express themselves physically through hairstyle and makeup, but to also help them reveal their authentic inner beauty. Through conscious conversation, a Beauty Maker can help a client tap into yet unexpressed, creative, and sometimes hidden parts of their authentic being. A Beauty Maker's goal is the deliberate integration of your clients' inner and outer beauty towards whole life wellness.

A Note About Affirmations

Our words are so powerful. Our words have the power to change things. The wisdom of the power of words has been passed down for centuries. It has been said that all of the world was created through thought, word, and then deed.

We are creators of our own worlds, and so it is essential that we become aware of how we use our words moment to moment. This is where affirmations come in handy. They are intentional phrases meant to train our subconscious minds to a higher vibration of thought that will help create the improved life we desire. Remember, thoughts will come and go, but you always have a CHOICE! When you decide which words you choose to keep and which ones to release, you become the creator of your life.

I LOVE affirmations! I was first introduced to the concept by motivational author and metaphysical lecturer, Louise Hay, over 20 years ago. Louise says to affirm something is to "declare it to be true." And YES, affirmations work…when YOU work them!!

It is important to say affirmations OUT LOUD and even write and rewrite them in your journal pages. As your subconscious HEARS the new information, over time it will begin to integrate the deep changes necessary for positive change.

"Every single thought I have and every sentence I speak is information. It is either positive or negative. Positive affirmations create positive experiences, and negative affirmations create negative experiences. If I continually repeat negative statements about myself or about life, I produce more negative experiences. I now rise beyond my old habit of seeing life in a negative way. My new affirmation is to only speak of the good I want in my life. Then only good will come to me."

"In the beginning is the word."

LOUISE HAY

You Can Heal Your Life. Bath: Camden, 2008. Print.

find your center

The Power Of Touch

"Too often we under-
estimate the power
of touch, a smile,a kind
word, a listening ear,
an honest compliment,
or the smallest act of
caring, all of which
have the potential
to turn a life around."

—LEO BUSCAGLIA

A wise Beauty Maker once said:

Never take for granted the power of touch. Only a handful of professions in the world are given a license to touch people. Commit to using touch with exquisite awareness, with only positive intention and deep care.

affirmation

Today as I touch my own hand
to my heart, I remember to bring
positive intentions and love
to myself as well as those
whom I touch.
I know my touch
has the power to heal.

Humans are social creatures, and we all need a certain level of physical contact. There is much research done about the healing power of touch. Touch has been proven to decrease blood pressure, increase white blood cell count, decrease anxiety, improve sleep, and increase endorphins.

- Pay attention to how you feel when someone with whom you are comfortable shares a touch with you—a hug from a child; a loving touch from an old friend; a sweeping hand across your back from a partner... Really notice what goes on in your body and mind.
- Imagine a day with absolutely no physical contact of any kind. Now imagine, a week, a month, a year. What would that be like for you?
- How do you use touch with clients and family?
- Who are your clients who live alone and perhaps lack sufficient physical contact? How can you help them heal when they are in your chair?
- Be aware of your touch style—is it light, soft, abrupt, firm, fast? Make sure you know what kind of touch brings joy to your clients.
- Imagine how important your caring touch is to that person and consider how meaningful your connection is the their health and well being.

The next time you touch someone—whether it is a client, your child, a spouse or your dog—take a minute to be sure the intention behind your touch is clear and be sure to make it a positive one filled with love and care.

How to practice the Power of Touch:

- As you stand behind your client to consult on a hair style, lay your hands on his shoulders, softly or firmly, depending on what you know about your client's preference.
- Pay special attention to those clients who you know are lonely or do not have many people in their lives. Take the time to listen closely to their stories. Give them an extra long hug goodbye as they leave. You will benefit from the healing power of touch as well!

I Am At Your Service

"The best way to find yourself is to lose yourself in the service of others."

—GANDHI

A wise Beauty Maker once said:

Know that you are a gift to your clients. They love, and appreciate the special way you make them look, and feel beautiful—both inside and out. Authentic heart-centered service touches the soul.

affirmation

I am filled with love and gratitude
for my clients today.
It is my honor to serve them
with awareness and joy.
In serving them well,
I also serve myself
and the universe.

Consider your role as a Beauty Maker. What does it mean to you to serve?

- Do you fully honor your role as a service provider?

- How do you feel when you get exceptional service at a restaurant, hotel, or event?

- Imagine four ways you can enhance your client service to make your clients leave feeling the same way you did when you experienced exceptional service. List the ways.

Ask your clients how you can better serve them in the salon. Give them choices, receive their input and make it happen for them!

How to practice Service:

- Keep a small blanket in the salon for chilly days.
- Provide a hot cup of tea or a cold glass of water.
- Have a favorite magazine ready and waiting.
- Spend some time thinking about a change for specific clients, (even those who typically don't like change) in between visits, grab a photo off the internet or sketch out your idea.
- Text or e-mail your client that you're excited to see them and have some new inspiration to share!
- Have mints, candy, snacks to share at your chair.
- Offer your client a choice in the background music if its possible. When possible play soft mood music.
- Diffuse essential oils for relaxation or energizing. (Check with client for scent sensitivity)
- Send a birthday or holiday message to a client.
- Offer information about a special service or product that you know will make a difference in your client's health and style.

My Thoughts Are Powerful

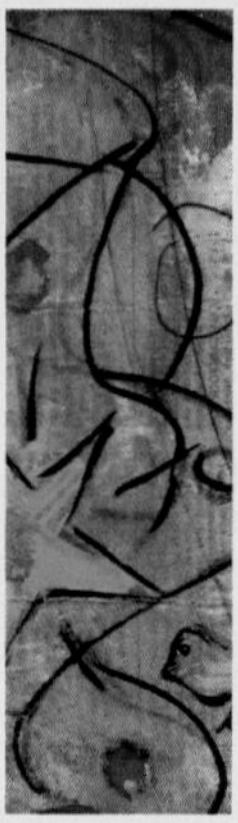

"A man is but the product of his thoughts. What he thinks he becomes."

—GANDHI

A wise Beauty Maker once said:

The energy and attitude you bring to your day, whether positive or negative, will be mirrored back to you in the reflection of others. Your energy and attitude will make your reality what it is. You are that powerful.

affirmation

Today I choose my attitude.
I am happy, light, and grateful.
I know I can choose my thoughts,
and I will use my mind to bring joy
to myself, as well as
to inspire others.

It can be easy to blame other people for your foul moods, but when you do this, who holds the power?

- How does it feel to take ownership and responsibility of your mood, attitude, energy level?

- How does it feel when you project positive thoughts into a conversation or situation?

How to practice the Power Of Thought:

Step away from the perceived problem for a moment.

- Get some fresh air.
- Create and use a power move that gets the blood flowing and reminds you that you're in control. Example: hands on hips, back straight, feet firmly planted, breathe— think Wonder Woman or Superman.
- Put a smile on your face (though you don't feel like it) and fool your brain into thinking you're happy. It's a proven technique and it works!
- Take a five minute break. Close your eyes and in your mind go to your "happy place". Come back and start fresh.
- Consciously change your energetic vibration with aromatherapy—use pure essential oils that help clear out negative energy: orange, lemon, peppermint.
- Be a role model for your clients: Invite them to select an essential oil to help them clear out their frustrations; offer a short mindfulness podcast and headset while they are waiting or during the session; remind them of a positive memory or experience they shared with you in a previous visit.

You can decide in every moment to take your power back and change your thoughts and attitude to change your life. Know how to get back to your happy place? Use the **My Thoughts Are Powerful Worksheet on page 104** to transform your negative thoughts to ones of peace and joy.

The Law of Attraction

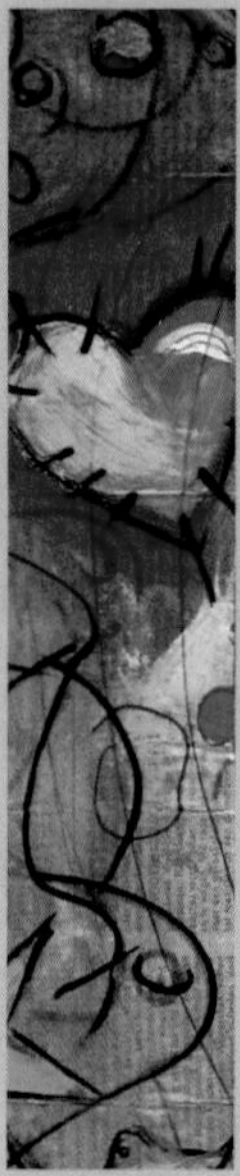

"Be thankful for what you have, you'll end up having more. If you concentrate on what you don't have, you will never ever have enough."

– OPRAH WINFREY

A wise Beauty Maker once said:

You will attract to you what you are, not what you want. Become the very thing you wish for your life, and watch the magic of manifestation become yours. You are the creator of your world.

affirmation

Today I allow the goodness of the universe to enter my life. I will happily receive all that is mine.

There is a clear alignment between our beliefs and the quality of our lives. If you believe something is possible, then it becomes possible. If you don't believe it is within your power to obtain, it is not very likely that you can have it.

- Be mindful of your own thoughts. If there is underlying negativity, where is it really coming from?
- What are some new feelings or beliefs you can conjure up to better reflect a positive outlook? We do this to better align with the vibration of the best vision you have for yourself. You will attract what you are. Good vibes attract good vibes. People, places and things.
- What is on your big wish list for the universe? Can you readily articulate the items?
- Are you waiting for these things to appear with worry or concern? Or are you embracing positive thinking and creative visualization to move towards them?

How to practice the Law of Attraction:

- Create a collage of images and words that you clip from books and magazines to help you clarify your intention about what you want to attract into your life. Use your vision board regularly and add to it as you are inspired. Put your vision board where you will see it everyday. It will become a source of inspiration and enthusiasm to move towards what you truly want in your life.
- Instead of waiting for your boss to tell you that you've done a great job, approach her with sincere gratitude and appreciation for your job. Be authentic and really feel appreciation in your whole body. Give the thanks you want to get and watch it come right back to you.

Practicing the Law of Attraction is simply about turning conscious intention into positive action. For step-by-step guide, check out the **Law of Attraction Worksheet on page 105**.

Self-Acceptance

"To be beautiful means to be yourself. You don't need to be accepted by others. You need to accept yourself."

—THICH NHAT HANH

A wise Beauty Maker once said:

You must get to know your own magnificent, innate beauty in order to truly know and value another's.

affirmation

Today I see myself as valuable.
I know my true nature
is joyful and loving.
I love and approve of myself
exactly as I am.

Self-acceptance is a big topic. The best place to start is to find out who you really are before you try to change you.

- What do you really want people to know about you?
- What makes you unique?
- Name five qualities your parent, best friend or client would say about you. Which of these things do you believe whole heartedly about yourself?
- Write the qualities that describe your true authentic self.

How to practice Self Acceptance:

- Before you apply your makeup or wash your face in the morning look in the mirror, peer deeply into your eyes and see your inner four-year-old self. Tell her that you love her, accept her, and there's nothing she can do that will ever change that. Repeat daily.
- When you hear a client get down on herself (I *should* have gone to the gym...I *should* have gotten a promotion...), remind her of something wonderful about herself. See her through the eyes of love.

Remember: The more you criticize yourself, the less you see your true self because the ego self or false self, gets in the way. The most powerful way to undo the effects of self-judgment is through practicing self-kindness. Forgiveness and kindness bring you back to your authentic self and innate goodness. Take a break from self-improvement and enjoy some self-love! For step-by-step guide, check out the **Self Acceptance Worksheet on page 107**.

Haut auftragen und trocknen lassen. Den Testst...

...ihen auf der Haut belassen. Wenn es zu keiner Haut...

...werden. Im Fall einer allergischen Reaktion Nicht a...

...ei späteren Anwendungen nicht zu allergischen Rea...

...Stunden, Juckreiz oder Ausschlag den betreffende...

...t nicht weiter verwenden. Vor erneuter Verwend...

...ie Verstärkung der allergischen Reaktion zu ve...

...Colorationscreme in einem nichtmetallischen...

...Artego Peroxide OZ 3% (10 Vol) nur bei Ve...

...% (20 Vol) deckt graue Haare ab und hellt bis zu 2...

...(12%) ...

...bis 40 Minuten. **Anwendung:** immer auf das tro...

...r Haar, das noch nie gefärbt wurde: Tragen Sie di...

...der Haare auf. Beginnen Sie ca. 2–3 cm entfernt v...

...einwirken, dann tragen Sie die Farbe am Ansatz auf...

...einwirken. **Für Haar, das bereits gefärbt wurde:** Tra...

...die Farbe 25–30 Minuten einwirken. Wenn notwendig v...

...er und tragen die Farbcreme auf die Längen und Spitze...

...5–10 Minuten einwirken oder noch besser gleichen Sie d...

...ssen Semi-Permanent (Tönung) Sortiment ohne Ammoniak...

...**Shampoonieren:** Spülen Sie die Creme mit warm...

...t und shampoonieren Sie das Haar anschließend mit Artego...

...von grauen Haaren: 100% Deckkraft erreichen Sie imme...

...Cold Natural Nua... ...von kurzer Verwendung von Mo...

...den vor dem Auftragen ist. Beispiel...

...gilt auch für Kunden, die bereits...

...inen kleinen Bereich in der Ellbogen...

...ieine Menge des Produkts...

...schließend dem gewünschten Farbt...

...ine kleine Menge der Mischung auf d...

...Mischung 48 Stunden unterbrox...

...nimmt, kann das Produkt angewendet...

...Test ist keine Garantie dafür, dass es b...

...Bei Hautreaktionen wie...

...abspülen und das Produkt...

...Mischen Sie das...

...Teilen (1:1) mit dem gewünschten...

...auf. Tonhöhe auf. Stellt bis zu 1 Tonhöhe auf...

...9% (30 Vol) deckt graue Haare ab...

...tragen, niemals vorher waschen. Farbe...

...die mittleren Längen und Spitzen...

...die Farbe 20–25 Minuten...

...Creme weitere 30–35 Minuten...

...Ansatz auf und lassen Sie...

...die restliche Farbe mit Wa...

...die Coloration weiter...

...zorgvuldig gereinigde... ...gebr...

...Als u medische onderzoek...

...overgevoeligheid voor een...

...nnen veroorzaken. Bewaar de verf...

...ndervindt.

...dige gevoeligheidstest. Wij raden...

...deling te doen, zelfs met klanten die...

...een gedeelte in de elleboog of achter het...

...ak een kleine hoeveelheid van de verf...

...vold door het kleur recept dat u wilt gebruike...

...Breng een kleine hoeveelheid van het kleur...

...gedeelte niet wassen of afdekken en laten rus...

...de substantie 48 uur zitten. Als de huid...

...deling toepassen. Als er wel een reactie...

...niet dat er geen allergische reactie...

...Als de huid een allergisch...

...ary tattoos may increa...

...pplied on customers:...

...oloring products b) wh...

...ical condition (eczema...

...inform the consum...

...raindications...

...the risk of allergic reactions...

...rsons under 16 years of...

...who previously have had...

...scalp is sensitive, irrit...

...psoriasis, facial...

...ut the co...

...the...

Spill
open
Allow
today

Be Brave

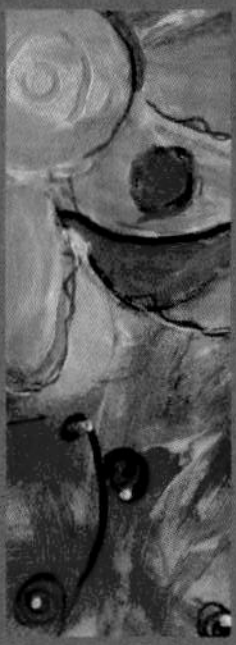

"Life begins at the end of your comfort zone."

—NEIL DONALD WALSH

A wise Beauty Maker once said:

If you do not risk, you may never know the most magnificent parts of yourself that lay waiting to be discovered.

affirmation

I am brave and bold.
I step beyond the known
to discover magnificent beauty
waiting in myself.

- What scares you? Speaking in public? Flying in airplanes? A last-minute color correction on a 16 year old on Friday at 4pm?

- What is something you would like to do, but don't think you can? You know, where you say: *Oh, I could never do that!*

- What would you risk by trying to do it?

- What would you gain?

Think about a brave person you personally know. What attributes do they have that makes them brave?

Do you share any of these qualities with this courageous person? If so what are they? Be honest with yourself.

How to practice Being Brave:

- Try techniques you think you are not good at, like updos, perms, freehand balayage, or ombre, etc...

- Take that class you are interested in.

- Pursue your business idea.

- Take yourself out to a movie.

- Travel alone— so empowering.

- Stretch your palete— try new foods you think you don't like.

- Suggest the style or color that you know will look amazing on your not-so-into-change client.

- Ask your boss for a raise or more time off. Or both!

Creativity

"Whatsoever you do,
if you do it joyfully,
if you do it lovingly,
if your act of doing it
is not purely economic,
then it is creative."

—OSHO

A wise Beauty Maker once said:

The source of your creativity is endless. Be the vessel through which the endless source flows and add your unique beauty to the world.

affirmation

**My creativity flows freely.
It's fun and easy to create.
I'm an artist and the world
is better for
my unique contributions.**

- How do you express your creativity?
- Remember a time that you were at your most creative. What were the circumstances that enabled this creative flow?
- Who are your creative heroes? What do you think feeds their creativity?
- What prevents you from being your super creative self?
- Are you waiting for more time, space or approval? Give yourself permission to be creative NOW.
- What is one way you can be creative this week at work or at home? Commit to that one creative act by the end of the week.

View each client as a canvas. Take the opportunity to use your creative touch to bring out your client's unique beauty. Let them walk out looking and feeling like your masterpiece.

How to practice Creativity:

- Take time to practice new edgy techniques on a mannequin head, friend or colleague.
- Get inspired! Visit a museum, subscribe to an art magazine, check out other contemporary artists on Instagram, Pinterest, etc.
- Approach daily tasks with a creative mind—cook with unusual ingredients and fun presentations, style your own hair differently in the morning, rearrange the furniture in your home or work space.
- Display local artists on the walls of your salon. For step-by-step guide, check out the **Creativity Worksheet on page 106**.

Abundance

"Abundance is
not something
we acquire.
It is something
we tune into."

—DR. WAYNE DYER

A wise Beauty Maker once said:

Abundance and fortune are yours right now. All you must do is live in gratitude for what you have already, and give to others the feeling of abundance you wish to know.

affirmation

Today I give of myself to others,
knowing there is enough
to go around.
I allow the universe
to fill me with
its abundant gifts.

- How have you engaged in a scarcity mentality, where opportunities are few and anxiety and worry reign?

- How can you flip scarcity and fear into an abundance mentality, full of opportunities?

- What you focus on will manifest. So focus on abundance, not scarcity.

Stop focusing on what you don't have and be grateful for and enjoy what you currently have. Take note of what you appreciate, and watch the magic of the abundant universe flow towards you.

How to practice Abundance:

You get what you give when there are no strings attached.

- Buy a cup of coffee for the car behind you in the takeout line.

- Give your client a free product 'just because'.

- Send a note of thanks and appreciation to a client, co-worker, friend, salesperson or anyone who might least expect it.

- Give a little more than you think you can to a charity or person in need.

- Start a giving campaign at your salon. One day a month donate all of your tips to a local charity. Promote this in the salon so your clients can deliberately participate in the flow of ABUNDANCE!

Mindfulness

"Mindfulness means paying attention in a particular way: on purpose, in the present moment, and non-judgmentally."

—JON KABAT-ZINN

A wise Beauty Maker once said:

Be mindful in your thought, word, and deed, so as to be present in your life and available to the NOW. Now is the only time there is.

affirmation

I am mindful in my thoughts,
my words, and my actions.
I am attentive and
present in my own life
and available to the now.
Anything is possible when
I am fully in the now.

Think about what it means to be fully present.

- When was the last time you had a truly mindful moment and what did it feel like to
  be in that state of awareness?

- How do you feel after a long day of rushing and pushing to get to the next client?

Don't get me wrong, you can still be busy with a full book of clients and be mindful at the same time. The beauty of incorporating mindfulness into your busy day is that it awakens your senses and helps you enjoy each moment, each client, each conversation. Life is richer.

- What can you do today to give yourself a mindful moment or two?

How to practice Mindfulness:

- Give 110% of your attention to the color, viscosity, fragrance of the hair color as you mix and apply it.
- Be a full observer as you sweep the floor and wash hair.
- Build a mindful moment into your appointment. Be present. Look directly at your client, touch her shoulder and ask if there is anything you can provide to make her more comfortable. Allow space to answer. The important piece is that your client feels that you are truly present with them.

Add a moment of awareness each day: Stop what you are doing and center yourself with 3–5 slow, deep breaths. Feel your feet firmly on the ground, your chest rising and falling with each breath. Savor the serenity of the moment for itself. Bring your breath and attention back when thoughts and to-do lists creep in. Notice them and then let them go. No judgment or criticism! Then, carry on, with a more centered energy to your day. You will start to cultivate your mindfulness muscle and it will grow over time until it becomes a natural part of your vibe. People will be drawn to your new energy.

Resilience

"If you're trying to achieve, there will be roadblocks. I've had them; everybody has had them. But obstacles don't have to stop you. If you run into a wall, don't turn around and give up. Figure out how to climb it, go through it, or work around it.

—MICHAEL JORDAN

A wise Beauty Maker once said:

It's not what gets you down that matters,

it's how you respond and get back up that counts.

affirmation

I don't let the challenges of today hold me down.
I know there is always tomorrow.
I choose to be resilient and strong.
I am hopeful. I have faith.
I am resilient.

Recall a challenging time, where you thought things would never get better.

- What external resources did you use? Some examples of resources: friends, family, books, activities.

- What internal tools or assets did you draw on? Some examples of assets: courage, faith, persistence, patience.

Know what tools you have and which you lack. Strengthen your assets by using them. Work to acquire new tools. Recognizing the assets and resources in your resilience toolbox will help you access them in future difficult times.

Which type of person are you—a Barbicide jar half-full or half-empty?

You can be a victim of circumstance or you can use your toolbox. You get to choose.

How to practice Resilience:

- Celebrate bouncing back from something challenging in your life, no matter how large or small. Treat yourself to something special to honor and reinforce the asset that got you through the tough time.

- Recognize when your client shares a story where he demonstrates resilience. Celebrate his particular asset or resource: self-confidence, determination, joining a support group, asking a brother for help, etc. Make sure to thank him for reminding you of the importance of resilience.

PEACE

Self-Care

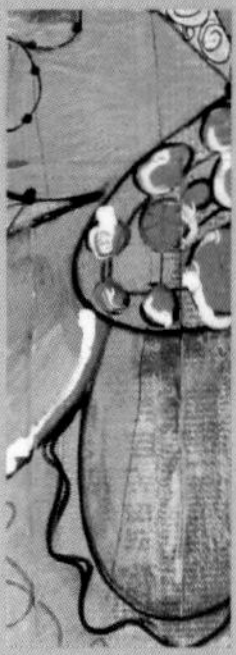

"If your compassion
does not include
yourself,
it is incomplete."

—JACK KORNFIELD

A wise Beauty Maker once said:

It is never selfish to care for your own needs. We must make sure our well is full before we can offer our water to those who are thirsty.

affirmation

I lovingly care
for myself and my needs.
I can offer help
from a full heart
and nurtured soul.

• What do you do to honor and take care of YOU—physically, spiritually, emotionally?

• What prevents you from more consistent self-care?

• Do you believe you're worthy of your own self-care?

List 10 self-care activities you would enjoy. Example: walking in the park, dinner with a friend, monthly massage, dancing, having someone else do your hair for you on a day off, etc.

• What's one thing you can do today to start to show yourself compassion, love, and self-care?

Be honest with yourself about any addictive behaviors you may have adopted such as smoking, food, drugs, alcohol, work, exercise, TV/media. Look online for fellowships, groups and organizations in your area that can help you get healthy once and for all.

You are SO very worth it... and YOU are NOT alone. Addiction can be lonely. A NEW YOU is a choice, and it is ONLY YOU who can make it. Give yourself a gift and start TODAY.

As service providers it is imperative that we give ourselves permission to care for SELF so that we may sincerely care for others. Your soul knows the difference between selfish and self-care.

How to practice Self-Care:

• Sit down to eat a good lunch even on a busy day at the salon.

• Spend regular time with friends who feed your soul and vice-versa.

• Get a massage or go for a walk after dinner.

• Show appreciation to your client for being so consistent with her appointments and her self-care. Be curious and start a conversation about other ways in which she practices self-care.

Joy of Movement

"Physical fitness is the first requisite of happiness."

—JOSEPH PILATES

A wise Beauty Maker once said:

Our bodies were meant to move, play, and dance. Get out from behind the chair and stretch, dance, or walk every day.

affirmation

**I love to move my body
in different ways.
My body willingly responds
with strength and flexibility
when I get up and move!**

- When does your body feel strong and flexible?

- What prevents you from being more active?

- What will you commit to this week, to start on the path to a more active lifestyle?

How to practice Joy of Movement:

- Research shows that even short spurts of cardio exercise can impact cellular health, mood and energy. Design a five minute routine that you can do between clients or find an app to guide you.

- Offer easy movement to your clients before, during and/or after a cut. No need for fancy yoga moves. Guide your client in a simple shoulder roll to release tension. As he leaves the chair, have him stretch his arms above his head. Tailor the exercises to meet the abilities of your clients.

- Have an impromptu dance party! Just crank the tunes and dance your pants off for 20 seconds or 20 minutes at the beginning, middle, or end of your day.

- Check out YouTube videos or books on Chi Gong or Tai Chi.

- Take the stairs

- Walk, walk, walk—as much as you can everyday. Even if its just a few more feet, it adds up!

- Set the health monitor on your phone or get an exercise app to keep track of movement and get accountable!

Conscious Conversations

"For beautiful eyes, look for the good in others; for beautiful lips, speak only words of kindness; and for poise, walk with the knowledge that you are never alone."

—AUDREY HEPBURN

A wise Beauty Maker once said:

Your words are very powerful. Be careful how you use your words. Before you speak ask yourself: Is it true? Is it necessary? Is it kind? If not, then silence is best.

affirmation

Today I choose to revel
in the silence
unless what I have to say
is true, kind,
and necessary.

- Think about a time you said something that you wished you didn't say. How did you feel once you realized that you couldn't take back what you said?

- Be truthful with yourself about whether you are generally a positive influence or a negative influence. Reflect on the energy you bring to a conversation.

Talking a lot isn't necessarily negative, but we must have awareness when our conversations are too much.

How to practice Conscious Conversations:

Find something on which to compliment each client this week. Be authentic. See how good it feels to be a positive influence in someone else's life.

Model conscious conversations by choosing NOT to gossip. Start positive conversations with your clients who tend towards gossip. Some conscious conversation topics:

- Favorite childhood memories.
- Upcoming or past travel experiences.
- Love story about meeting partner/spouse. Everyone loves to share this story.
- Funny pet stories.
- Community service work and opportunities.

For step-by-step guide, check out the **Conscious Conversations Worksheet on page 108**.

Silence Speaks

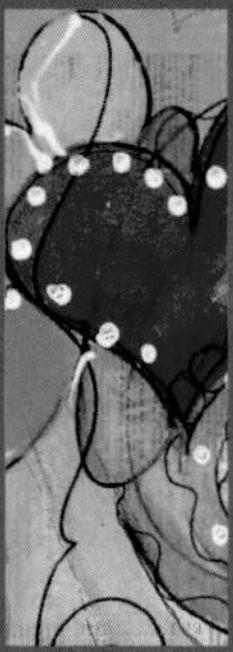

"Silence is the language of God, all else is poor translation."

—RUMI

A wise Beauty Maker once said:

Deep beauty can be found in the sacred space between things. Settle into that space as often as you can, and you will find peace and love.

affirmation

Today I will not be afraid
to allow space in my life.
I will look for the beauty
in between the words, thoughts,
and actions of my day.

It is said the universe whispers to you in the silence between your thoughts.

- Recall a time when you were intentionally silent, whether in prayer, meditation or walking in nature. How did you feel in the silence?
- Have you received whispers from your God, Spirit, or any other force you feel a connection with in the universe?
- How did you feel when you connected to something beyond yourself?

It is important to allow space in your life for this connection to take place. Whether you call it prayer, meditation, or connecting with nature, make time in your life for it so the universal powers can help guide you. Go with the flow. It doesn't have to be so difficult. Just be quiet. Allow. You can't hear when there's too much noise.

How to practice Silence:

- Take five minutes before you arise from bed in the morning to lay silently, just being with your breath.
- At night before you close your eyes, focus on your in and out breath for two minutes. See what the silence says to you.
- Take a silent walk in nature, or a drive to work with no radio. Enjoy the scenery. Breathe deeply.
- Offer silence as an option on the menu of things to "do" while waiting for a color to process. Sometimes if it's not offered, a client won't choose it.

The more space you make for silence, the louder it speaks.

- What could you do this week to allow more silence in your life?
- Will you commit to practicing silence for just a few minutes each day?

Body Love

"And I said to my body,
'I want to be your friend',
it took a long breath
and replied, 'I have
been waiting my
whole life for this.'"

—NEYYIEAH WAHEED

A wise Beauty Maker once said:

Our body is our most precious gift. It works best when fueled with wholesome, nutritious, natural food and drink and plenty of sleep.

affirmation

**Today I choose to eat healthy and drink plenty of water.
I love to take care of my body.
I appreciate my body's beauty and strength.**

- Has there been a time when your body did not work the way you wanted it to, due to sickness, neglect or injury?

- If your body could speak out loud to you, what would it tell you it needs from you?
  BODY: I need _____ .
  (More rest, more activity, healthier foods, less alcohol, less stress, more sleep, etc.?)

- What are two ways today that you can show your body more love?

How to practice Body Love:

- Take time to massage your skin with some great natural body cream, or the perfect essential oil blend after your shower or bath time.
- Provide samples of great products for your clients to try in the spirit of body love.
- Provide wholesome snacks for your colleagues and clients like nuts, fruit, baby carrots.
- Honor your clients for being good to their bodies. When you hear they have stopped drinking diet soda, are walking in the morning or going to Pilates, etc., make sure they hear that you honor their efforts to be healthier.

Play

"Play is the highest form of research."

—ALBERT EINSTEIN

A wise Beauty Maker once said:

All work and no play make us very tired and grouchy. Re-learn how to play and get happy!

affirmation

Today I allow my inner child
to come out and play.
I will not judge, or criticize.
I will play in joy, and
laugh with abandon.

Remember a time you allowed yourself to be goofy, take risks, and make mistakes. What were you doing?

This is play, we used to do it naturally as children, before the monster of self-consciousness took over.

- What makes you feel playful, relaxed, silly, at ease?
- What's one thing you can do today that would help you tap into that playful part of your personality again?

Remember play is an activity for the sake of the activity not about the outcome. Whether you're "good" at it or "bad" or somewhere in between, doesn't matter. Play is about enjoying the moment, being free and expressing yourself.

Whatever PLAY is for you, do it today, this week, and for the rest of your life! When people forget to play they get depressed, weary, sick. Play, play, play, play, play and then play some more!

How to practice Play:

- Buy a coloring book and crayons. Put your favorite music on loud, and color outside of the lines if you want!
- Have game night at your house for salon staff.
- Organize a kickball game.
- Take salsa dance class or cha-cha-cha!
- Encourage play in your salon. Have adult coloring books, brain games, anti-stress balls, and puzzles available for clients to play.

Connections

"Connection is the energy that is created between people when they feel seen, heard, and valued."

—BRENÉ BROWN

A wise Beauty Maker once said:

Your clients are the heart and soul of your business. Take the time to see them as whole people. Listen to their stories with all of your heart and share yourself. It is through these connections that true beauty is made.

affirmation

Today I understand
my clients are in my chair
for more than just a haircut.
Our connection is valuable.
I see their true whole beauty
inside and out
and they see mine.

- Notice how you connect with friends, coworkers and strangers. Are you open? A good listener? Do you hug? Shake hands?
- How do you connect with clients behind the chair?
- What was the most meaningful client connection you have made and why was it so meaningful?

As Beauty Makers we obviously connect to our clients through our license to touch. But our healing force goes beyond the physical, and thus we can connect more deeply. We make clients look and feel great. We listen. We validate. We share. We serve. Clients return again and again because we can make them feel truly beautiful. We have that capacity. Of course we mustn't forego professionalism, but life is real, and it's messy, and making authentic connections is the golden opportunity of the Beauty Maker. It is what makes us special. So if life plays out while your client is in the chair, be real, be open, let the connection run both ways. Trust is the cornerstone of all lasting personal and professional relationships and is formed when authentic selves are shared.

True healing is part of the Beauty Maker's job behind the chair. My wish for you is that you experience the magic of connection and how it transforms lives.

Some important reminders:
- Boundaries are critical. Discern which clients invite connection from those who simply want the technical service.
- MINDFUL sharing can prevent the dreaded oversharing.

How to practice Connections:

- Connect FULLY with receptive clients.
  See them: look them in the eye. Hear them: listen authentically. Touch their shoulder or arm to convey the connection.
- When vulnerability is shared, offer a safe, nurturing space. Follow up with a call or email acknowledging the connection and thank them for their authenticity. Keep it simple but real. Don't try to be the hero. Just convey your understanding that life can be messy and it's ok to be vulnerable.

Teamwork

"If everyone moves forward together then success takes care of itself."

—HENRY FORD

A wise Beauty Maker once said:

Get over yourself already, it's not always about you! Work as a team in your salon and watch your life and salon grow.

affirmation

Today I see myself
as part of the team.
I know my contribution
will lend itself to the strength
of the salon and
success for everyone.

- Think about teams that you have been a part of, whether in sports or for work projects. What was needed to reach your goal as a team?
- What is challenging to you when working as part of a team?
- In what ways are you a team player at work? List five ways.
- In what ways could you be more of a team player at work? List five ways.
- How could you improve the overall teamwork in your environment?

How to practice Teamwork:

- Offer help to a coworker who seems to be in the weeds.
- Anonymously wash the color bowls and dishes in the sink.
- Fold and sweep without being asked.
- Organize movie night and other fun team-building activities outside the salon. Teams need to play too.
- Make sure clients see that there is a collaborative team in the salon. Introduce your colleagues and create an inclusive environment.

Time Management

"Either you run the day, or the day runs you."

—JIM ROHN

A wise Beauty Maker once said:

Time is an illusion, a state of mind. If you think you won't have enough of it this will be true for you. Use time wisely, don't let it use you.

affirmation

Today I will have plenty of time
to give great service.
I will work with ease, and joy.
Time works for me.

Take a close look at your time-related patterns and habits.

- Are you an early bird or a late Lucy? When did this pattern start? Why do you think this is so?
- Do you have trouble staying on schedule behind the chair with clients?
- What issues have been caused by poor time management?
- How do you feel when you are running behind?
- How do you feel when you are on time or early?
- Be in charge of your time by planning wisely and honoring your plan. Sometimes life happens and we need to be flexible too.

Choose to be stress free and happy. Take back your power.
Be on time for your beautiful life!

How to practice Time Management:

- Set your alarm clock 15–30 min earlier to start your day with some wiggle room. The key is not to squander the time away doing unnecessary things.
- Take a hard look at your appointment book. Are you allowing enough time for each client's needs? While you may think you need to cram as many clients in as possible, think about what you will gain by providing optimal service because you are not rushing and anxious about time.
- Set a gentle alarm to notify you 15 minutes before the next appointment time. It's OK to let your clients know that you are doing this. Perhaps it will inspire them to be more timely.
- Talk less and listen more. Get that client out the door! (Hey, I made a rhyme!)

What are some other time management strategies that work for you?

Create
xox

Beginner Mind

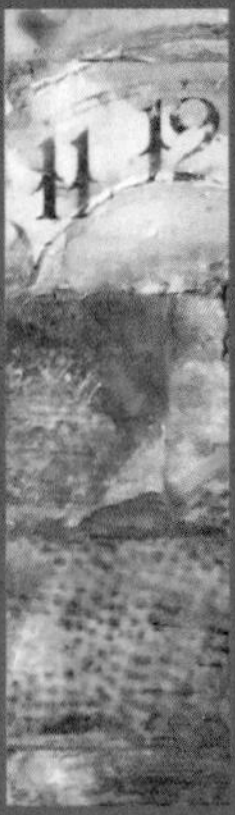

"In the beginner's mind there are many possibilities, but in the expert's there are few."

—SHUNRYU SUZUKI

A wise Beauty Maker once said:

Never forget how to be a student in life. There is always something to learn, and you will always be surprised at who can teach you.

affirmation

Today I will put aside what I know, so that I will be open to learning new and interesting ways of being, doing and seeing.

- Whether you have been practicing your craft for 3 or 30 years, there is still plenty to learn. Think about the last time you learned something new—a technique, modality, way of presenting your ideas, how to use a new electronic device. How did it make you feel to be a newbie again?

- Is there something you secretly want to learn, but have not pursued? If so what is it and what is stopping you?

- Be honest with yourself. We can often get in our own way because we don't want to risk looking inept.

There are loads of reasons we can stop ourselves from opening up to new learning opportunities. When you tap into your Beginner Mind you will be surprised at how much you will gain by softening to the flow of incoming information.

How to practice Beginner Mind:

Step out of the "I know, I know" flow and take the stance of "What can I learn?" Put aside the beliefs you already have for a little while, and try something new without expectations.

- Ask a coworker to teach you that great technique you have seen him do on his clients.
- Sign up for that class that looks interesting to you.
- Be more open to learning new things from your clients. Having them share their expertise with you will add to their Beauty Making experience.
- Say Yes to everything for a day and see where the yes takes you. (Be smart, don't get yourself in any danger of course!) If you have a great adventure and learn something new, do it again. If you don't do it again anyway!

Breathe

**"Breathe. Let go.
And remind yourself
that this very moment
is the only one you
know you have
for sure."**

—OPRAH WINFREY

A wise Beauty Maker one said:

Our breath is our life. Be mindful of your breath throughout your day. If life in the salon gets hectic, just remember to breathe and suddenly it will get calm again. Repeat as needed.

affirmation

Today I will be mindful
of my breath
as I work with my clients.
I will converse, cut, color,
sweep and breathe
with ease and joy.

Are you breathing right now? I'm sure you are, but did you have to stop and think about it? Most likely your answer is yes.

Without breath we do not exist, yet we rarely give thought or thanks to this miraculous flow that keeps us vital. Our breath is a measure of our presence. When we are afraid we instinctively hold our breath. If we are conscious of our breath and mindful of its benefit to us, we can have the upper hand on worry, anxiety, and stress.

How to take a mindful breath: Close your eyes and slowly take a deep breath in through your nose. Fill your lungs completely and then slowly exhale through your mouth. Empty your lungs gently and completely. Repeat two more times...and as needed throughout your day.

You may notice a centered focus and calmer vibe now. Do this daily and whenever you find yourself feeling overwhelmed or anxious. You will gain a sense of balance that will help keep things in perspective. If you can make the mindful awareness of your breath your constant companion, you will have an anchor that will ground you whenever you need it.

How to practice Breath Awareness:

- Upon waking, before you rise out of bed, take three mindful breaths. Give thanks for the gift of a new day and for all of the possibilities that lie ahead.
- Encourage your clients to focus on their breath during a shampoo or treatment or even when sitting in the chair processing. Guide them by taking some deep, audible breaths yourself. Using aromatherapy with essential oils is a great way to compliment mindful breathing.

Self-Worth

"When you get to a place where you understand that love and belonging—your worthiness—is a birthright and not something you have to earn, anything is possible."

—BRENÉ BROWN

A wise Beauty Maker once said:

You are not what you do, you are not what you have, you are not what others think of you. You are far more than that. You are made of the same molecular stuff as the stars, the galaxies and the entire universe! Simply put, you are one of the most natural things in the universe, and you belong here as much as the sun and the moon!

affirmation

Today I recognize
my innate worthiness.
I know that I am lovable, valuable,
and nothing I do, or don't do
can change this fact.
I belong.

Self-worth is about valuing your inherent worth as a person.

- Do you think you have a high or low sense of self-worth? Why do you believe this is so?
- Was there a time in your life that your self-worth was higher or lower? What happened to change this view?
- Do you have a loud inner critic? What does s/he say?
- How might your beliefs about your self worth be holding you back?
- How does your self worth manifest at work? Are you charging what you could be for your services?

Lack of self worth can manifest as mild to extreme dysfunction in our personal relationships. If you feel you are in a mentally, emotionally or physically abusive relationship you must tell a friend, co-worker, minister, doctor or call an abuse hotline immediately

How to practice Self-Worth:

- Meditation can help manage critical inner dialog that only serves to undermine your sense of self-worth.
- Contribute to something meaningful to add meaning to your life.

Volunteer in your community in an area that is important to you. Studies show that volunteering increases a positive sense of self-worth.

Be generous. Giving and helping others increases our sense of self-worth. Just make sure your giving is balanced with good self-care!

- Call the "friend" who has been treating you like garbage and say that you have decided to take "a break" from the relationship until you can agree on how to have a healthier one.
- Notify your clients of your new prices and that you sincerely appreciate their business.
- Find support. Enlist the help of a coach or counselor to help you deal with unresolved issues. Take good proactive care of your soul's needs!

For step-by-step guide, check out the **Self-Worth Worksheet on page 109**.

A Solid Foundation

"Be sure you put your feet in the right place, then stand firm."

—ABRAHAM LINCOLN

A wise Beauty Maker once said:

When your feet are supported, they can carry you all day in your aim to make whole beauty for your clients. Be kind to your tootsies and wear good shoes!

affirmation

Today as I dress for work,
I will remember
to start with my feet
and work up.
Happy feet equal
a happy day.

- What kind of shoes are you wearing right now? Are they supportive and comfortable? Could you walk a few miles in them? Seem like a random question? It's not!

As beauty/spa/health professionals, we are on our feet 8–12 hrs a day, and that can take a toll on our bodies. If you are in your 20's or 30's you may not feel it, but if you plan on having a long career I highly suggest you wear the most supportive (and of course cutest) shoe you can afford. Often back issues start at the foundation — our feet! As busy professionals we cannot afford to be laid out with back issues, so better safe than sorry, don't you think?

At the end of a long day I have found myself tired and cranky, not because I messed up a color correction or because my last client was a no-show, but because my FEET HURT LIKE *$#@!! Be smart and put your best, most supportive foot forward.

- How do you hold your body all day?

Notice your body positioning while you are working. Stay grounded through your legs and feet, and strong through your core. Keep your shoulders relaxed and your heart open. Remember to breathe!

Also make sure you are standing on a supportive matt, not on concrete or another hard surface. And use the hydraulic chair. It's your buddy!

How to practice a Solid Foundation:

- Get fitted for sole inserts at your local running store. Then use your specially designed support in a variety of cute shoes!
- Consider therapies like massage or chiropractic services to support you in maintaining your healthiest foundation.
- Take alignment yoga to learn how to align your body for strength and vitality.

A Good-bye

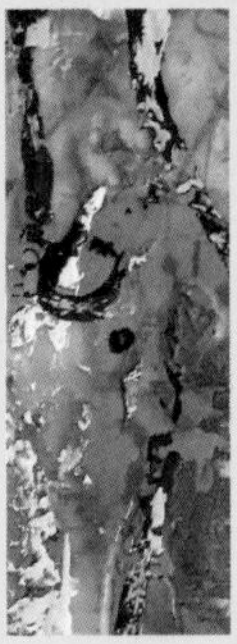

"Don't cry because it's over, smile because it happened."

—DR. SEUSS

A wise Beauty Maker once said:

Clients are with you for a season or a reason. Sometimes when a client leaves after being with you for a while it's because the season has changed, sometimes there is a reason, and sometimes it's not even about you.

affirmation

Today I will remember that clients are with me for a reason or a season. I will enjoy them, and I will let them go with ease.

Think about the varied clients who have come and gone in your salon.

- Have you ever begrudgingly taken on a new client who at first you thought was a "difficult one", only to look back years later and realize she is one of your most loyal and favorite clients now?

- Has the opposite situation ever happened to you? A new, seemingly easy-going client sits down and ends up being the bane of your existence?

- Have you had a wonderful client who seemed to love your service, just never return? How did this make you feel?

- How do you behave when you see an ex-client out in public? Do you happily and confidently speak to them, or do you run and try to hide behind the baked beans display?

I have personally lived all of these experiences and I tell you my life is so much better when I can just smile because it happened. We can't please everyone all of the time. We can only do our best. We must stand our ground in a professional way with some clients, admit our shortcomings with others and not beat ourselves up when a client chooses to leave.

How to practice Goodbye:

- Write a brief, heartfelt note to the client who has not returned. Tell them you were thinking of them and appreciated their business. Wish them well. Say goodbye. Expect nothing. Be at peace. Move on.

- Send an e-mail or hand written note to your top five most loyal clients and let them know that you appreciate them. Do this with the intention that if they left you tomorrow with no explanation you would be at peace.

worksheet
MY THOUGHTS ARE POWERFUL

In order to extract yourself from a negative mindset or environment, it's good to know how to find and get back to your happy place. Here's a short visualization exercise to get you started.

Sit quietly and close your eyes.

Think of something that brings you great joy—a place you love to visit, a dear friend with whom you always feel happy to be around, a holiday or event.

Once you have your vision, describe it in detail in your journal.

How tall is this friend and what is s/he wearing? What is s/he doing—smiling, laughing, singing?

What is going on around you? Can you feel the warmth of the sun? Can you see a lake or river or majestic mountains? What sounds do you hear?

How do you feel in this beautiful place or with the people you love? Peaceful? Accepted? Open? Loved?

Breathe this feeling in deeply and exhale any lingering negativity.

In your mind's eye, wrap this scene up in a gift box with a fancy bow. Put it in safe corner of your mind. Remember, this gift is always there for you—you can unwrap it anytime you need to shift your thoughts and attitude towards peace and joy.

worksheet
LAW OF ATTRACTION

Imagine what it is you are wishing to attract into your life—a new job, a healthy relationship, a new car, peace, joy, more fun, new friends. Know that it is possible to have ALL that you desire, but first you must invite your desire into your life and really feel it. If it's peace you want more of in your life, you must be peaceful within yourself first. If it's abundance you are seeking it is wise to tune in to the feelings of being grateful for all you already have. This is the way to attract the new energy of the things, situations, relationships, abundance which you desire.

Practice tapping into the Law of Attraction flow.

Meditate for 5–10 minutes. Relaxing your mind will increase brainpower and a sense of open positivity. Simply sit, and focus your attention on your breath. Watch your breath rise and fall and when you lose track of it (which you will, everyone does) and find yourself in a thought again, kindly return back to the breath just noticing that you were distracted. Continue until you feel calm and more centered.

Be super clear about what you want. Make your big wish list for the universe in a dream journal, or on a vision board. (cutting and pasting images, words from magazines, books, etc) that are in line with your vision, in order to make the desires more concrete.

Make your specific request to the universe and write it down. Really visualize it happening in as much detail as possible. Write your wish down in the present tense as if it is happening right NOW: "I am so grateful and joyful that...I have this, ...am doing this, ...am earning this much and can be on this lovely vacation, ...am giving this much to charity, etc."

Feel the feeling of having or being the thing, or attitude you desire. Accessing the feeling state will dramatically change your frequency and start the process of attraction. Think, speak, and act like it is already true. If you want more joy, be joyful, if you want more money, feel gratitude for the money you currently have, if you want better relationships, be a better friend, spouse, etc.

Remember to include gratitude. Be thankful for what you already have: all the simple and big joys in your life, all the ideal and not-so-ideal clients who choose your service. Be thankful for what you are trying to manifest as if it has already arrived.

worksheet CREATIVITY

Sometimes we need a re-set. This visualization will help you to see and feel the awesomeness of YOUR creativity.

Read the following scenario and then close your eyes and imagine it really happening to you.

You walk into the salon to start the week. You're having a great morning and feel wonderful in your body and mind. The sun is shining. Your first client is on time and sitting in your chair waiting for you to make some beauty magic. She says, "I was so excited to come and see you today, I loved my last cut and color! I am wanting a change today. I trust you, and I want you to use your creativity to do absolutely anything you want to my hair. You're the artist! I promise I will like anything you do. The sky's the limit and money is no constraint. I'm your canvas."

After some time and great conversation, your masterpiece is complete. You spin your client around to face the mirror. She sees her reflection and expresses authentic delight, "Oh, my gosh I LOVE IT! Is that ME? You are a genius!" She is glowing from the inside out. Your chest swells with joy from making her feel so beautiful. You are on top of the world. You are exactly where you're supposed to be, doing the work you're supposed to do, with the clients who are supposed to be sitting in your chair. You are at your most creative and enjoy life to the fullest. You can't wait for tomorrow to do it again.

Know that this is how great it can be when you set your creative self free in the salon.

worksheet
SELF-ACCEPTANCE

With self-acceptance, it's important to understand yourself before you accept yourself. This exercise guides you to visit yourself as a child so that you can see your sweet self without the layers of criticism, shame, anger, etc. that can build over time. Become a dear friend with your inner child.

Close your eyes and visualize yourself as a small child around the age of four.

See this small child sitting on a park bench alone in the sunshine.

Now picture your adult-self coming down the sidewalk to greet your four-year-old self. Say hello and sit next to yourself. Hold your own small hand. Look deeply into your own four-year-old eyes.

Your inner child is waiting to hear what you will say. What does she need to hear in order to feel wonderful about herself? Allow yourself the time to allow the truth to surface.

Go ahead and say it out loud now. Breathe.

Continue looking deeply into your four-year-old eyes. See her truly as she is, as a unique individual deserving of unconditional love. Allow her to feel your genuine caring deeply in her heart.

When you are ready, tell her you love her. Thank her for being there for you and make sure she knows that you're always there for her too. Say goodbye for now with the knowledge that you can easily find each other again.

Slowly come back to the present moment. Breathe deeply.

Journal about your experience.

worksheet
CONSCIOUS CONVERSATIONS

Do you need to make amends to anyone for a time when you were not at your best or kindest?

What would the you who knows better now have said?

Even if it was years ago, it's not too late to make amends.

Can you remember a time when you withheld engaging in a conscious conversation. What kept you from doing so?
- Self-consciousness?
- Self-doubt?
- Worry about seeming inauthentic?
- Lack of the right vocabulary?
- Extreme self-editing?

Call that person up, write a letter, send a text. Regardless of how you do it, simply acknowledge that you may not have been your best self at that moment. They may not respond but believe me they will appreciate the outreach and may even grow themselves from the experience.

Be a better you. Be brave and try it!

As we grow we realize words are very powerful. As we mature we realize keeping to our own business, raising people up, being an inspiration, and simply being kind is what propels us and the people around us to new heights. This helps the world to be a better place. Negativity only breeds more negativity. Be the bright light you were meant to be and SHINE!

worksheet
SELF-WORTH

Some of us have been exposed to painful experiences and attitudes in childhood. If not addressed, these can become part of our belief structure, and as adults we may accept their destructive viewpoint as our own.

If your inner coach is constantly comparing you to others or criticizing your actions, you need to fire that coach! Replace that inner critic with one who can see you authentically with your own feelings, desires and values.

It may be time for you to begin rewriting the script of your life to include forgiving yourself and others for misgivings of the past. This is one way to boost self-esteem and self worth so that you may begin to live a more grateful, mindful life in the present.

Do you wonder why you acted against your own best self-interest? *Why did I yell at him about that? Why did I stop going to the yoga class I loved so much? Why didn't I study for the exam?* The critical inner voice leads us to self-sabotage. It sees us through a negative viewpoint based on a past event and steers us away from our true goals and desires.

Take a mindful moment to breathe and relax yourself as you've learned to in the previous chapters. If you wish, you may look into a mirror while you repeat these words out loud to yourself:

> *I forgive myself for my mistakes. All people make mistakes. I used to feel regret about some of my mistakes because I am a good person and want to do the best that I can, and now, I am still a good person and I release the feelings of regret because I have learned and moved on. I forgive myself for errors I have made, because I have felt bad about them long enough. I have suffered enough, and now it is time to be free. By freeing myself from past mis-takes, I can move on and do good things. I forgive myself.*

Andrea Saccone Snyder is a visual artist, Beauty Maker and Life Coach.

Andrea has made art, spirituality, self growth, and beauty her life's work for as long as she can remember.

As a Hairstylist I get to make each head of hair my canvas. I am a sculptor, colorist and architect. I not only touch people's hair, I get to touch their hearts, and soul's, as well. When a client walks out of the salon, they look and feel beautiful, each is a unique masterpiece! Behind the chair she's recognized the need for people not only to express themselves through their hair/appearance, but through integrating all the beautiful parts of their personalities.

"Working on a clients inner-self is as important, if not more important, than working on the outer self."

"I've discovered that through acquiring the valuable skill set of coaching, I'm able to guide my clients through the process of self discovery, revealing the true integration of self which they truly desire, Clients are connecting with the flow of their unique inner and outer whole beauty. It's magic to see!"

Andrea is owner of FLOW Beauty, and founder of The FLOW Beauty Project, which empowers salon pro's and woman of all types to integrate inner /outer beauty while reclaiming their most creative selves. A third generation stylist/owner with a background and education in the fine arts, Andrea has 25 years in the beauty industry. Andrea has trained in beauty in places like London, NYC, and Toronto, CA. She currently makes her home in beautiful Chatham County, North Carolina where she paints, writes, coaches and makes beauty everyday. Andrea is a trained RCA life Coach and brings this skill set, along with her love of beauty, spirituality, and self growth to the chair and beyond. She is always equipped to inspire whole life beauty, or what she calls "Flow Beauty – beauty from the inside out". This is a book to help empower you, to help grow you from the inside out, This is a book to help you help those whom you touch everyday live a life full of Flow Beauty.

Thank you for reading and sharing this little book
with your friends and loved ones.

Additional copies may be purchased at
amazon.com

To schedule workshops, courses, retreats
or presentations that will help make
yours and others lives more beautiful
both inside and out,
please visit:
www.theflowbeautyproject.com
or
www.themindfulbeautymaker.com

Join the Mindful Beauty Maker Tribe

In Peace and Beauty,
Andrea xo

35421140R10071

Made in the USA
Middletown, DE
06 February 2019